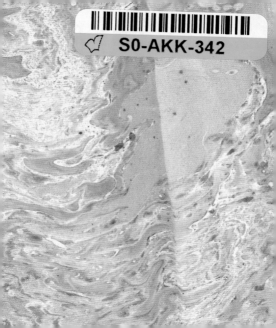
S0-AKK-342

A Little Book
of *Dreams*

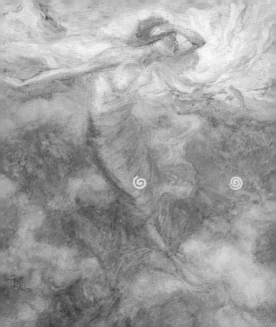

A Little Book of Dreams

Randy Burgess

Ariel Books

Andrews and McMeel
Kansas City

Marbleized endpapers by Lisa A. Mahmarian

ISBN: 0-8362-1051-4

Library of Congress Catalog Card Number: 95-80739

Contents

Introduction

We all know what it is to dream; every night it happens to each of us, as we forget the outside world and drift separately into our private kingdoms. And yet no one truly understands this mystery—not our most famous psychologists, our wisest scientists, our most dedicated researchers.

What do dreams mean? That depends, it seems, on what you want them to mean.

To Wilhelm Griesinger, an early explorer of psychology, dreams were nothing more than madness. "In insanity, as in dreams, all idea of time is

wanting," he wrote. "Minutes seem hours. . . . The dreamer, like the insane, accepts all."

Sigmund Freud, at the turn of the century, decided that all dreams were about sex. His fellow psychologist Carl Jung disagreed, maintaining what we are more likely to believe today, that dreams are about self-discovery.

Dreams can be fun, heartbreaking, or silly. You can fly out of the window and up into the sky, talk in languages you don't even know, visit places and people long forgotten in your waking life. Some dreams even seem to provide a glimpse into the future.

Whether or not you believe that dreams should be taken seriously, whether or not you believe they can help you find wisdom and creativity, the pages that follow will delight your imagination. In them you'll find the history, folklore, psychology, and magic of dreams—and perhaps a hint or two to help you solve your own nightly riddles.

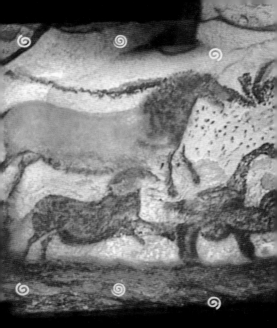

Dreams of the Ancients

We may never know what prehistoric peoples thought of their dreams, or whether some of the paintings chalked upon the walls of caves were meant to depict not merely the world seen in daylight but the even stranger world glimpsed between dusk and dawn.

It's clear, however, that early peoples did regard dreams as glimpses of another world, often a divine one. The ancient Egyptians, for example, believed that the gods communicated to them through dreams. Dream visions were so

highly prized that Egyptian priests developed spells to bring them forth.

One such spell instructed the would-be dreamer to draw a portrait of the god Besa in ink upon the left hand. Before going to bed, this hand had to be wrapped in a black cloth. The dreamer had to maintain absolute silence prior to sleeping, refusing to talk to anyone or answer any questions. Furthermore, a petition asking for the dream had to be written by the light of the setting sun, using an ink that included among its ingredients the blood of a white dove, frankincense, myrrh, cinnabar, mulberry juice, rainwater, and the juice of wormwood.

The Greeks and Romans knew that although some dreams might be genuine visions, others were more like stories. "Sometimes," wrote the soothsayer Artemidorus in the second century, "there are Dreams which cannot possibly happen; as when you dream that you fly, have horns, go down into Hell, and the like: These are Allegorical."

The ancient Chinese, meanwhile, believed that everyone had two souls, one connected with the body and the other with the spirit. The second, spiritual soul was the one involved in dreams; each night it left the body to communicate with spirits in the land of the dead. Because the soul needed time to return to the body, care was taken not to wake a sleeping person suddenly. Even today, in some regions of China, alarm clocks are still regarded as potentially dangerous.

Prophetic dreams are frequently mentioned in the Bible, as when God granted Solomon's gift of wisdom in a dream. Another example is Jacob's dream of beholding a ladder extending from earth to heaven, with angels climbing up and down the ladder's rungs. In the dream God announced that Jacob's offspring would spread throughout the world; the ladder can be seen as a metaphor expressing a profound and otherwise invisible connection between the two worlds, holy and material. Dreams often speak in such visual metaphors.

Two Theories:
Freud and Jung

Probably the most widely recognized authority on dreams in the popular American consciousness is still Sigmund Freud, the turn-of-the-century inventor of psychoanalysis who has had so much influence on the way we look at ourselves in general.

Many of us assume that Freud was the one who invented the idea of the unconscious—that part of ourselves that we normally aren't aware of, and that emerges in dreams. Freud himself considered his text on dreams to be a pioneering advance over everything that had gone before. "My presumption that dreams can be interpreted at once puts me in opposition to the ruling theory of dreams," he announced proudly.

And yet, as critics have since pointed out, philosophers as far back as Plato had known that our irrational side could appear to us in dreams. And many authors before Freud had written on the presence of a rich visual language, including sexual symbols, in dreams.

So what did Freud come up with that was so different? Put simply, he managed to convince people that dreams seem crazy to us because they are disguised messages about sex. The messages have to be disguised, Freud went on, because our sexual desires are so infantile they frighten us; an internal censor rewrites these scary thoughts into a series of riddles, which only highly trained (and highly paid) psychoanalysts can unravel.

Freud's chief rival was a Swiss psychologist named Carl Jung, whose influence has been nearly as great as Freud's—in almost the opposite direction.

Jung didn't agree with Freud's theory of self-censorship. "The dream is a natural event," Jung wrote, "and there is no reason under the sun why we should assume that it is a crafty device to lead us astray."

Jung saw the seemingly chaotic nature of dreams as our unconscious speaking in its natural language, which relies less on words and more on symbols. Some of these symbols seem to be universal, and can be found in folklore and

religion around the world. For example, Jung believed the circle was often symbolic of wholeness and balance, as it is in much of Asian art.

Jung also believed that dreams are best interpreted in a way that makes sense to the individual dreamer. In this view, dreams about people close to us sometimes express concrete concerns or problems, rather than anything elaborate or concealed. Historical or mythical figures, meanwhile, are best understood as expressing some aspect of ourselves.

Because dreams so often tell us about ourselves, they can be used to spur insight and personal growth, Jung said. Today, relatively few people talk about the universal archetypes Jung was so fond of, but many dream theorists echo his conception of dreams as potentially creative and liberating.

Common Dream Themes

Modern dream interpretation has evolved to a point beyond Freud and folklore. Today, we no longer believe that objects or people in our dreams automatically harbor certain meanings, regardless of the individual dreamer. Modern dream interpretation depends on developing a personal dream vocabulary, rather than relying on generalizations.

Still, people are similar enough for common themes to emerge from our nighttime adventures—and even a few common symbols. Try pondering the following themes and symbols; they can help unlock your imagination and teach you to start thinking about the specifics of your own dream language.

Falling

Dreams of falling are commonplace, whether they involve tall buildings, mountains, unexpected pits in the ground, or other scenarios.

Going beyond the obvious observation that the falling dream is generally a frightening one, some experts say falling is usually a metaphor for worry about failing in a real-life situation. Perhaps we fear we are falling down on the job, or have lost our balance on some issue. We may feel we're in danger of losing our social status or our emotional security. We may associate falling with unethical or immoral behavior on our part—hence the old phrase "a fallen woman."

Popular author and psychologist Ann Faraday says that people who dream of falling should make sure they aren't neglecting some important task. In some cases, Dr. Faraday contends, the dreamer's worry could concern something quite literal, such as an unsafe railing on a balcony. Any scary dream, in fact, should always be examined first for literal meanings of unsafe or hazardous real-life conditions that the dreamer may have been ignoring.

Being Chased

This is similar to the falling dream, in that the dreamer usually feels helpless, unable to stop events from happening. Many chase dreams turn into the scariest of nightmares unless the dreamer is able to influence the course of events, by escaping or even by waking up.

A chase dream may mean that you feel at the mercy of some other aggressive person, or it may relate to feelings of guilt. One expert suggests examining your life to see if you are feeling a conflict with a particular person; you may want to share your dream with that person, or ask if he or she is angry at you for some reason you're not aware of.

Occasionally, the people you are fleeing in your dream may represent some aspect of yourself that frightens you.

Nudity

Discovering in a dream that one is naked or semi-

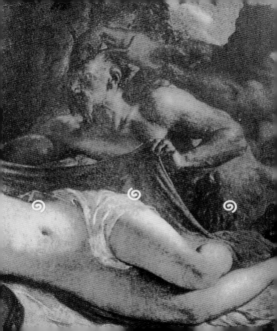

naked in a public place is also common. Usually these dreams do not have a sexual connotation—they seem to be more about embarrassment or lack of preparation than anything else.

Some researchers speculate that the dreamer may be worried about what people would think if they knew of the dreamer's real feelings or abilities. This might happen, for example, if a person is worried that despite success in life, he or she is a fraud and will soon be found out.

One way to unravel all this for a particular dream is to examine where the dream takes place—if the setting is at work, at home, or someplace else. Also, ask yourself what clothing might represent for you in that situation—whether it be inhibitions, behavior as imposed by others, or some other outer layer.

Examinations

One of the most disconcerting dreams is finding yourself back in the classroom at school, about to take a test, and knowing that you are completely unready and will fail without doubt. If we really are in school, then such a dream may be alerting us to do a better job of preparation. If we're not in school, however, we may be expressing a fear that in some other way we are being tested. Rather than see this as a generality about your life, try to connect it to specifics: perhaps there really is some circumstance in which your preparation isn't adequate and you need to do a better job.

The Body in Dreams

Parts of the body can take on special significance in a dream. The head often symbolizes thought and identity; the face may symbolize the personal image we present to the outside world, as opposed to who we are inside. Dreaming of wearing a mask might imply that you are secretly hiding your true thoughts. A dream about acne or blemishes on your face might mean you're feeling guilty about something. If you can't see your face in a dream, it might mean that you are unwilling to recognize some aspect of yourself, such as a strong emotion you would rather not be feeling.

The eye is significant in dreams because sight often takes on a double meaning. For example, dreaming that you can't see through a window because of mist or dirt on the panes might mean that you are having difficulty seeing the truth about a situation. Dreaming that you're blind could mean the same thing.

Hands are important in dreams, too, because we often talk about whether we can "handle" a situation or not; if our hand is hurt in a dream, it could mean we're afraid we've lost control or can't cope in some way. Conversely, great dexterity in a dream could mean that we are feeling confident about our ability to tackle a problem and solve it.

Losing Teeth

Loss of teeth in a dream may have to do with fear about damage to some actual part of the body (perhaps it's time to make an appointment with the dentist!), but it may also be a metaphor for another kind of loss. For some, loss of teeth may mean loss of face in certain social situations. Others may connect teeth with biting and aggression, so that the loss of a tooth is connected with feebleness, helplessness, or an inability to convey anger. Again, think about what teeth represent to you.

Sexual Dreams

Sexual dreams can be interpreted literally, especially if, in the dream, you are attracted to a particular person from waking life. But they can also be interpreted metaphorically, as expressions of energy or excitement about some other issue that isn't sexual at all. Be particularly on the lookout for metaphorical possibilities if the person involved in your dream is a well-known figure of some kind, since these people often stand for attitudes and feelings we have about ourselves, rather than for specific individuals.

Water

Water means different things in different dream contexts, but often it is connected to the unconscious, to the mysterious forces of life that go on beneath our everyday awareness.

For example, if we dream of diving, this may mean that we want to discover our deeper feelings about a situation.

The sea can represent a mothering, nurturing place, in which we are bathed and renewed, or it can represent something dangerous, even life-threatening. Streams and rivers, on the other hand, are usually restful, and may suggest a renewal, a return to your fundamental self.

Weather

In books and movies, weather often expresses mood: the bad guy rides into town in a Western, and suddenly the sky darkens and the wind whips up as if a storm is coming.

The same sort of thing can happen in a dream. The invisible producer who arranges our dreams sometimes stages unhappy feelings of being unloved or unable to love in wintertime, with snow or ice on the ground and a chill in the air. As always, though, be careful to take your individual beliefs into account: if you love to ski or just plain enjoy cold weather, then dreaming of snow could mean happiness, not sadness! Likewise, dreaming about hot weather could be bad or good, depending on your personal associations.

Food and Drink

The connection between food and love is deeply rooted in the human psyche. We even use expressions that vividly express this link, such as "starved for love." In dreams, then, food will often have deeper significance.

A hearty meal, a feast, may mean the dreamer's emotional life is rich and well-nourished. Dreaming of hunger, on the other hand, could mean the opposite. If you share a meal with someone in a dream, that may indicate that you feel especially close to that person.

Drinking usually carries a similar connotation of emotional nourishment—although the specific meaning will vary depending on what is being drunk. For example, alcohol suggests excitement and the relaxing of sexual inhibition, whereas milk is more likely to be interpreted as satisfying or pacifying.

Birds

Birds have been powerful symbols of the human soul for thousands of years, perhaps from the notion that the soul is lighter than the physical body and rises through the air at death, during sleep, or in moments of ecstasy.

Specific birds might represent the soul's capacity for either good or evil. A bird like the dove may symbolize gentleness and spirituality; the raven or crow can signal darker aspects. The eagle is noble and ruthless; the peacock, beautiful but self-absorbed.

Attacked by Animals

Because we live in a civilization where attack by wild animals is no longer a major concern, being attacked by an animal in a dream rarely corresponds to a real-life threat (unless you live next door to a particularly ferocious dog). Instead, such dreams may be about "wild" impulses or emotions that we find threatening, either within ourselves or displayed by others in our life. For clues to the nature of these feelings, ask yourself questions about the specific dream animal that attacked you. What qualities do you associate with that animal? Does it remind you of part of yourself, or of someone else you know, or of some conflict going on in your life?

Houses

A house in a dream, especially if it is not the house you currently inhabit, could represent either your self-image or your life as a whole.

If it expresses your self-image, then the front of the house might symbolize the outward aspects of your personality visible to others, whereas rooms toward the center or back might suggest less visible parts of yourself. The roof might stand for intellect and reason, the attic for memory, and the basement for the unconscious.

Dreams or nightmares about scary basements are common, and often reward thoughtful interpretation.

If the house represents your life, on the other hand, various rooms may symbolize various stages you've gone through. The stairways and hallways in between could be seen as connections between these different periods.

A house can even symbolize two lives, not one, as when it represents a marriage or relationship. The condition of the house may be a clue to your feelings about the relationship—whether it badly needs repair or is handsomely maintained; whether it has tidy, snug rooms, implying comfort and closeness, or spacious, large rooms that suggest an airy freedom.

Extraordinary Dreams

Nightmares

In psychologist Ann Faraday's view, nightmares often represent an aspect of the self with which we are uncomfortable and from which we would like to distance ourselves. We define that part of ourselves, in effect, as a shadow, a dark thing that isn't us, only to find that the shadow chases us everywhere we go. It may be our sexuality, our natural assertiveness, a part of us that was shaped by our mother or father, or some other aspect of the self that we have bent into the shape of a demon and can no longer recognize.

If you feel this may be true for a particular nightmare, try a bit of role-playing after you wake up, borrowed from Gestalt psychology: hold an imaginary dialogue between your dream self and the dream demon, in which each of you gets to express what you're feeling.

Another technique for overcoming nightmares has been adapted by various researchers from a Malaysian tribe called the Senoi. In the Senoi culture, according to Dr. Patricia Garfield and others, frightening dreams are transformed into friendly ones by remembering the cardinal rule that you must never run from a dream attacker, but always fight back. Dreamers who try this soon find themselves winning easily.

Once you're comfortable with this, you can not only fight back but even befriend your attacker! Ann Faraday used this tactic in one dream where she had been pursued by an enormous, ugly man intent on beating her up. She asked him what he wanted, whereupon he doffed his hat and invited her into a café to talk. He was only following her, he explained, because she was beautiful and he wanted to marry her. Upon waking, Faraday concluded that this ugly but powerful creature represented her own "brute strength and animal erotic energy," which she had always been reluctant to accept.

Flying Dreams

Since people can't flap their arms and fly away in

real life, it's surprising how often this ability is reported in dreams. We don't usually dream of other superhuman powers; why flying, then?

It's hard to know what the answer is, but there is no question that flying in dreams is usually associated with feelings of exhilaration and freedom. Some dreamers fly with their arms stretched forward like Superman; some lift off the ground and float weightlessly. Patricia Garfield reports one dream in which she flew with her hands on her car's steering wheel, even though she had left the rest of the car behind on the ground.

Many people learn to fly in their dreams during their childhood years. Mary Arnold-Forster, a well-known dream explorer who wrote a book called *Studies in Dreams* in 1921, recalled how she learned to fly in dreams to avoid a dark, scary staircase when she was very young. "It was then that the blessed discovery was made, and that I found that it was just as easy to fly downstairs as to walk; that directly my feet left the ground the fear ceased—I was quite safe; and this discovery has altered the nature of my dreams ever since."

Lucid Dreams

Closely related to the flying dream is an even stranger phenomenon—being aware that you are dreaming *while* you are dreaming! As those who have experienced them report, lucid dreams can feel fully as vivid as anything in waking life.

Usually, people become lucid dreamers by accident—they notice something unrealistic in a dream, question it, and realize that they must be

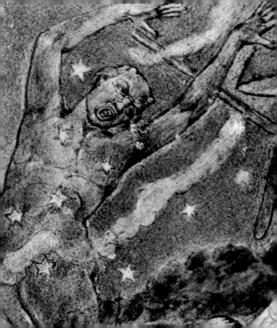

dreaming. They may also be so frightened by a nightmare that they try to wake up—which again leads to a realization that it's just a dream. Very often, flying dreams lead to lucidity, perhaps because of the intense pleasure and freedom involved.

As long as lucid dreamers hold on to the awareness that what they're experiencing isn't real, they can do almost anything. Dream researcher Stephen LaBerge has made the investigation of lucid dreams a personal quest. According to him, lucid dreaming becomes easier and easier with practice.

False Awakenings

Many people have had the experience of waking, only to realize that they are actually still dreaming. This is usually followed by a true awakening moments later.

Often a false awakening is filled with a kind of dread. For example, the dreamer may hear someone hammering on the door to the bedroom in a horribly threatening manner, as if a giant stood outside, about to burst in. Or, as another dreamer reported to C. E. Green, author of the study *Lucid Dreams:* "When I wake in this condition the whole room seems to be under tension. There is an atmosphere like an electric storm. Everything looks, somehow, as if it might fly apart."

Other false awakenings are much more gentle and usually involve the dreamer's testing to see if he or she is awake, and mistakenly concluding yes. False awakenings can sometimes lead to lucidity if the dreamer isn't fooled.

ESP and Dreams

At least one modern researcher, Robert Van de Castle of the University of Virginia Medical School, has concluded that if telepathy exists, it is more likely to take place between dreamers than between people who are awake. The dream-to-dream or unconscious-to-unconscious connection carries a powerful charge, according to Van de Castle, who has himself participated in dream-telepathy experiments.

In one experiment, he dreamed of a fishing scene on a boat. During the dream, a fish's face turned into a man's face. One of Van de Castle's partners in the experiment reported a startlingly similar dream that same night, in which she was on board a ship and a small whale changed into a man.

Dream Dictionaries

Dictionaries and other books providing ready-made interpretations for dreams have long been popular, dating back at least to *A Treatise of the Interpretation of Dreams*, published in 1601. In that work, readers were advised that "The sick person to dream that he married a maiden, signifieth death to ensue. But good it is unto him which beginneth a new business, for that it shall come into a good purpose."

Even without written books, dream events have been tied by folklore to specific meanings: losing a tooth means a death in the family, dreaming of a cat is bad luck, and so on.

These days, we may no longer believe in such easy answers to our dreams, but it's still amusing, and even thought-provoking, to ponder some of those old definitions and think about how they came to be. From various sources, then, comes this abbreviated dictionary of symbols, portents, cautions, and miniature prophecies. Read it with a grain of salt—but don't dream of salt, since such a dream is considered an omen of discord!

Abbot—To dream you are an abbot is a warning that plots are being laid for your downfall.

Acorn—If you see acorns in your dream, expect pleasant things ahead, with a great deal of gain. If you dream you're picking acorns up from the ground, that is a sign of success after much effort.

Alligator—As you might expect, it is not a good sign to dream of an alligator, unless you manage to kill it. Otherwise, this dream is warning you to be cautious.

Beer—If you like beer, then dreaming about it is a good omen, says one dream dictionary. Otherwise, if you dream about drinking beer in a bar it means you're in for a disappointment, or possibly that schemers around you are going to undermine all your hard work.

Carrots—Carrots signify that you are going to be prosperous and healthy. If you're a young woman and you dream about carrots, expect to marry young and bear many sturdy children.

Descent into a cave or abyss—Generally a descent into the underworld implies a journey into the unconscious, so as to retrieve and bring back to the light of day a valuable part of your personality.

Forest—As we might expect, a forest in a dream can often suggest uncertainty or obstruction, a lost path.

Horse—If a horse kicks you in your dream, this is a sign that your loved one is about to do something to make you realize you've made a mistake in choosing him or her.

Hyena—If a husband or wife dreams of a hyena, it signals misunderstandings and quarrels.

Lantern—Young women who dream about lanterns should be careful. A dream about a lighted lantern generally means you will marry well, to a charming, upstanding young man. If you should blow the lantern out, however, it means you will throw away your chance to marry such a man.

Leaves—A dream of green leaves on a tree often portends that you will inherit riches of one kind or another, or else that you will marry to your advantage.

Mansion—If you dream of being inside a mansion with a haunted room, this means you will suddenly come upon misfortune in the midst of happiness. Dreaming of a mansion alone means you will soon be wealthy. If you see a mansion in the distance, it also means you will be wealthy, but that it will take a little longer.

Map—Dreaming of a map means you are contemplating changing your life in a drastic way, but probably, in the end, for the better.

Newspaper reporter—If you dream of seeing a newspaper reporter, expect in real life to be annoyed soon by pointless small talk or petty quarrels. However, if you dream you are a newspaper reporter, that's an omen that you are likely to do some traveling quite soon.

Nymphs—To see nymphs bathing means that you will soon realize your most passionate desires. On the other hand, to see them when they are not bathing means disappointment. If you're a young woman and you see nymphs bathing, you will indeed realize your desires, but in the process you may violate society's sense of what is proper.

Onions—Dreaming of onions is a sign of spite and envy, but not necessarily on your part.

If you eat the onions, you'll overcome the spite and envy shown by others over your success. If you cook the onions, that means things will go quietly but well for you in business. However, if you dream of crying while you slice onions, your rivals will defeat you.

Parrots—A lot of parrots chattering away in your dream means that your friends are filling their time with idle gossip. However, parrots happily and quietly dozing signify a time of peace in your family. A dead parrot means you may lose some social contacts.

Picnic—Attend a picnic in your dream, and it's a signal that soon you'll find success and enjoyment in life. A storm during a dream picnic foretells an interruption of pleasure in real life, but only temporarily.

Scales—A dream about scales (the weighing kind) may tell you that you are on the point of making an important decision and are considering the pros and cons involved.

Trains—Dream of missing a train, and you may be missing an opportunity; catch a train, and it's a sign of vigor and progress. If you want to get off a train but can't, you may be afraid of reaching your destination. Arriving at a station can mean death.

Throat—Dreaming of seeing someone's attractive, graceful throat means that you will rise in your position in life. But dreaming that your own throat is sore means you'll soon be disappointed in a friend's conduct.

Trousers—A dream of trousers means you will be tempted to do the wrong thing.

Umbrellas—Dream of others holding umbrellas, and you will be appealed to for help in waking life. Borrow an umbrella in a dream, and you'll soon have a misunderstanding with a friend.

Vineyard—To dream of a vineyard or winery means either that you'll make a profitable investment on some risky speculation or that you'll shortly enjoy the delights of love. But a poorly kept vineyard indicates disappointment where you least expect it.

A Dream Sampler

Some dreams may even heal. This happened to
Stewart Alsop, a well-known political columnist
who, some years ago, was battling cancer. It was
spreading and his chances didn't look good.
Then one night he dreamed he was alone at
night on a train, which was about to stop at
Baltimore. When it did, Alsop looked out
through the door at what he presumed was the
Baltimore station—deserted, dimly lit, creepily
silent. As silent as death.

"We won't stop here," Alsop announced
loudly to whomever was in charge of the train
and the dream. "Start up the train, and carry on."

The next day, for the first time, Alsop's X rays looked better. The cancer had mysteriously begun to recede. Soon he was able to go back to work.

"There are mysteries," Alsop wrote later about his dream, "above all the mystery of the relationship of mind and body, that will never be explained, not by the most brilliant doctors, the wisest of scientists or philosophers."

Golfer Jack Nicklaus once suffered through a very bad slump that persisted despite all his efforts. Then one night he dreamed he had a perfect stroke with an entirely different grip.

"When I came to the course yesterday morning," Nicklaus told a newspaper reporter, "I

tried it the way I did in my dream and it worked.
. . . I feel kind of foolish admitting it, but it
really happened in a dream."

Nicklaus's scores immediately improved.

Mary Shelley, the author of *Frankenstein*,
first glimpsed her horrific creation in a dream.
In the summer of 1816, she and her husband
had been staying with friends at the Villa
Deodati on the shores of Lake Geneva. After an
evening spent in exchanging ghost stories, the
poet suggested that each of the group write a
horror story of his own. Mary Shelley went to
bed and had a terrifying nightmare.

"My imagination, unbidden, possessed and
guided me," she later wrote, "gifting the succes-

sive images that arose in my mind with a vivid-
ness far beyond the usual bounds of reveries. . . .
I saw the pale student of unhallowed arts kneel-
ing beside the thing he had put together—I saw
the hideous phantasm of a man stretched out,
and then, on the working of some powerful
engine, show signs of life, and stir with an
uneasy, half-vital motion."

Upon waking, she excitedly realized she had
been given her story: "What terrified me will
terrify others; and I need only describe the spectre
which had haunted my midnight pillow."

*A*s president, Lyndon Johnson often
dreamed of the difficulties he was struggling
through as the country's leader. In one recurring

dream, biographer Doris Kearns later recounted, Johnson would find himself in the Executive Office Building signing paperwork; he would rise to go home, only to discover his leg was chained to the desk. With a sigh, he would reach for another stack of papers and begin all over again.

Another recurrent nightmare possessed Johnson as the war in Vietnam intensified. In the dream, he would be lying on a bed in the Red Room of the White House, unable to move or speak; his body was transformed into the paralyzed, diminished frame of another president, Woodrow Wilson. To try to get over this dream, Johnson would walk through the dark corridors of the White House, carrying a flashlight, until he came to the place where Wilson's portrait hung on the wall. Touching the painting, he would reassure himself that he was not the man depicted therein.

A dream even helped Johnson decide not to run for reelection: In it, he was fighting to swim across a river to the bank, but couldn't reach it. He switched directions, fighting toward the other bank, but couldn't reach that either. Johnson found himself going around in circles—which, he decided upon waking, perfectly symbolized the impossible political situation in which he had become trapped.

Abe Lincoln apparently dreamed of his own assassination shortly before it occurred, according to his biographers.

In the dream, which he recounted to his

wife a week or so later, he found himself lying
in his bed in the White House, listening to a
deathlike stillness, which was soon broken by
the sounds of weeping in the rooms below.

Leaving his bed, Lincoln wandered from
room to room, unable to find who was crying;
the entire White House seemed deserted. Still
the sound continued.

Puzzled and alarmed, the dreamer continued
until he came to the East Room. With a shock,
he realized he had stumbled upon a service for
the dead. Before him lay a corpse wrapped in
funeral vestments. Soldiers stood on guard; the
sobbing came from a throng of mourners gath-
ered round.

Who, Lincoln demanded of one of the soldiers, is dead?

The president, the soldier answered—killed by an assassin.

Just then the crowd's grief grew excessive, startling Lincoln awake. For the rest of the night he could not sleep, but lay in his bed, worried and haunted by his vision.

*A*nother writer who found inspiration in dreams was Robert Louis Stevenson, the author of *Treasure Island* and *The Strange Case of Dr. Jekyll and Mr. Hyde.* Fancifully, Stevenson described his dreams as populated by elflike Little People, who were better at inventing plots than he was.

"Who are the Little People?" Stevenson asked himself. "They are near connections of the

dreamer's, beyond doubt; they share in his finan-
cial worries and have an eye to the bankbook . . .
they have plainly learned like him to build the
scheme of a considerable story in progressive
order; only I think they have more talent; and
one thing is beyond doubt, they can tell him a
story piece by piece, like a serial, and keep him all
the while in ignorance of where they aim. Who
are they, then? and who is the dreamer?"

Dreams fade quickly upon waking, as the
English poet Samuel Taylor Coleridge found
out to his regret.

In his preface to "Kubla Khan," Coleridge
explained that he had fallen asleep at his farm-
house while reading a book about the Mongol

emperor. Having nodded off, he began dreaming, and in his dream began composing beautiful poetry without effort. He composed two or three hundred lines in this manner, the images rising before his eyes translating themselves directly into words. Upon awakening, he eagerly found pen and ink and began at once to transcribe the wonderful things he had dreamed.

Then someone knocked on the door, a "person on business from Porlock," who kept Coleridge occupied for more than an hour. Upon returning to the epic he had begun, Coleridge was dismayed to find that, aside from the fifty-four lines he had set down before being interrupted, it was all gone. He couldn't remember a thing. The beauty of the five opening lines illustrates the magnitude of the loss:

In Xanadu did Kubla Khan
A stately pleasure dome decree:
Where Alph, the sacred river, ran
Through caverns measureless to man
    Down to a sunless sea.

Literary Dreams

Three times Randolph Carter dreamed of the marvelous city, and three times he was snatched away while still he paused on the high terrace above it. All golden and lovely it blazed in the sunset, with walls, temples, colonnades and arched bridges of veined marble, silver-basined fountains of prismatic spray in broad squares and perfumed gardens, and wide streets marching between delicate trees and blossom-laden urns and ivory statues in gleaming rows; while on steep northward slopes climbed tiers of red roofs and old peaked gables harbouring little lanes of grassy cobbles.

—H. P. Lovecraft, *The Dream-Quest of Unknown Kadath*

He opened his eyes and stared about very stupidly: a moment before he had been so solidly, so warmly and happily in Ireland, with a girl's hand under his arm, that his waking mind could not take in the world he saw.
—Patrick O'Brian, *Master and Commander*

After midnight dreams are true.
—Horace

Many's the long night I've dreamed of cheese—toasted, mostly.
—Robert Louis Stevenson, *Treasure Island*

*A*gain I find myself checking my memories as though they were facts. A dream does not take account of size. A puddle can contain a continent, and a clump of trees stretch in sleep to the world's edge. I dreamed, I dreamed that I was lost and that night began to fall. I was not frightened. It was though even at seven I was accustomed to travel.

—Graham Greene, "Under the Garden"

... Half an hour later the thought that it was
time to go to sleep would awaken me; I would
try to put away the book which, I imagined, was
still in my hands, and to blow out the light; I
had been thinking all the time, while I was
asleep, of what I had just been reading, but my
thoughts had run into a channel of their own,
until I myself seemed actually to have become
the subject of my book: a church, a quartet, the
rivalry between François I and Charles V.
—Marcel Proust, *Swann's Way*

But the most amusing times were when he and
she had a clear understanding that it was all
make-believe and walked through mile-wide
roaring rivers without even taking off their
shoes, or set light to populous cities to see how
they would burn, and were rude as any children
to the vague shadows met in their rambles.
—Rudyard Kipling, "The Brushwood Boy"

I dreamed I was in a strange city hunting for a man I hated. I had an open knife in my pocket and meant to kill him with it when I found him. It was Sunday morning. Church bells were ringing, crowds of people were in the streets, going to and from church. I walked almost as far as in the first dream, but always in this same strange city.

Then the man I was after yelled at me, and I saw him. He was a small brown man who wore an immense sombrero. He was standing on the steps of a tall building on the far side of a wide plaza, laughing at me.

—Dashiell Hammett, *Red Harvest*

At that very moment a cock crowed, and the weird procession vanished and left not a shred or a bone behind. I awoke, and found myself lying with my head out of the bed and "sagging" downward considerably—a position favorable to dreaming dreams with morals in them, maybe, but not poetry.

—Mark Twain, "A Curious Dream"

Once upon a time I dreamed I was a butterfly, fluttering higher and thither, to all intents and purposes a butterfly. . . . Suddenly I awoke, and there I lay, myself again. Now I do not know whether I was then a man dreaming I was a butterfly, or whether I am now a butterfly dreaming I am a man.

—Chuang-Tse

The text of this book was set in Bembo,
the display in Party and Koch Antiqua
by Snap-Haus Graphics
of Edgewater, New Jersey.

Book design by
Diane Stevenson of Snap-Haus Graphics

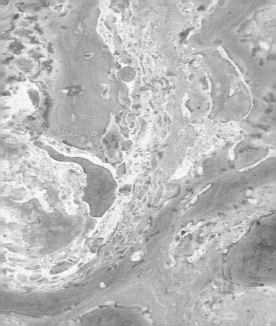